HEAVY WATER

Mario Petrucci

Heavy Water

A POEM FOR CHERNOBYL

ENITHARMON PRESS

First published in 2004
by the Enitharmon Press
26ʙ Caversham Road
London NW5 2DU

www.enitharmon.co.uk

Distributed in the UK by
Central Books
99 Wallis Road
London E9 5LN

Distributed in the USA and Canada
by Dufour Editions Inc.
PO Box 7, Chester Springs
PA 19425, USA

ISBN 1 900564 34 3

British Library Cataloguing-in-Publication Data.
A catalogue record for this book is available
from the British Library.

Typeset in Times Roman by Servis Filmsetting Ltd
and printed in England by
Antony Rowe Ltd

ACKNOWLEDGEMENTS

Take our words. Enrich them.
They are already active – but enrich them.

Books can step up to us – into us – in many ways. *Voices from Chernobyl* by Svetlana Alexievich was for me that rare precipitate force which calls another book into being. Its first-hand accounts of Chernobyl's aftermath, translated so remarkably by Antonina Bouis, are the central inspiration for *Heavy Water* and provide most of the source material and epigraphs. No acknowledgement can do justice to the courage and resolve of Alexievich, who was irradiated as a result of her work. Moreover, it is in *Voices* itself that its contributors continue to receive their most eloquent tribute.

I am blessed with friends generous with encouragement, constructive in their counsel: particularly Maura Dooley, Martyn Crucefix, Roselle Angwin, Rosemary Norman, Rob Pope, Tim Dooley, Brett Van Toen, Peter Brennan and Anne Prouse. They, collectively, have been the keen-eyed Argus for this manuscript. To Tanya, Rob, Ivan and Sasha I say 'ynam sknaht' – for the smorgasbord and antique chair which, together, supported an early warming of this poetry, right there round that hearth where Russian is spoken. I thank the Royal Literary Fund for successive Fellowships. Finally, I make plain my utter debt to Anne and to Peter for being so present throughout the birth of *Heavy Water* – for becoming, on the one journey, true companions.

*

A collection of excerpts from *Heavy Water* (entitled *Half Life*) won first prize in *The Daily Telegraph / Arvon* International Poetry Competition 2002. Extracts have been broadcast on BBC Radio 3 (*The Verb*) and have appeared in *Poetry Review, The Daily Telegraph, The London Magazine, The Arvon Journal, Poetry Nottingham International, Acumen, Agenda, Avocado, Anon, Soundings, Matter, Coffee House Poetry, Newswrite* (New South Wales Writers' Centre) and *Dream Catcher*.

Cover design: adaptation (by the author) of tracks generated by alpha particle radiation in a Cloud Chamber.

Every effort has been made to contact the editor and translator of 'Voices from Chernobyl' to apprise them of this project. Any correspondence would be most welcome.

SOME NOTES

Ukritye ('The Shelter') is the fourth reactor of the Chernobyl complex located at **Pripyat** in the Ukraine. It 'still preserves within its lead and reinforced concrete belly around 20 tons of nuclear fuel' (*Ogonyok* 17, April 1996; quoted in *Voices from Chernobyl*, Svetlana Alexievich, Aurum Press 1999, p.2).

Miners. At a critical stage following meltdown, liquid air was pumped under the reactor to freeze and stabilise the soil cushion. The speaker borrows from the patriotic song *May in Moscow*, often played on May 1st: 'The morning adds delicate colour to the walls of the ancient Kremlin ...' (*Alexievich*, p.118).

Directive 1A. Removal of contaminated topsoil around Chernobyl exposed a yellow-white sand characteristic of the area (*ibid.* p.88).

Soured Milk. 'You carry a coffin gently ... so it doesn't touch anything or hit anything. Otherwise, you have to expect another corpse.' (*ibid.* p.43).

Goluboy (literally 'light blue') is Russian slang for 'gay'. *Mal'vina* (a nickname among Russian gays) is a blue-haired puppet girl in the tale of Buratino by Aleksey Tolstoy.

This. Points to M H Abrams' *The Mirror and The Lamp*.

Olya. See Dante: *Purgatorio,* Canto XXVIII; lines 49–54. The quartered fruit, too, alludes to the Persephone myth.

Baba Nadya. 'She's a woman you call to come to your house when someone dies, to mourn, read prayers – she wept over the trees ...' (*Alexievich,* p.180).

Black Box. Various attempts to decontaminate vegetables and meat included making repeated changes of boiling water (e.g. *ibid.* p.46).

Bashchuk. 'We lay out the deceased on the door of his house. He lies there until the coffin is brought. I sat up ... all night while he lay on that door.' (*ibid.* p.32).

Roentgen: a measure of radiation exposure.

Heavy water: a form of H_2O based on deuterium, an isotope of hydrogen. Has a crucial role as moderator and coolant in some types of nuclear reactor.

Chernobyl is often translated as 'wormwood'. The root 'cherno-' denotes black.

CONTENTS

CHAIN OF DECAY

Lead 207   Stable
via beta and gamma radiation

Thallium 207 – 4.77 minutes
alpha radiation and x-rays

Bismuth 211 – 2.1 minutes
beta and gamma radiation

Lead 211 – 36.1 minutes
alpha radiation

Polonium 215 – 1.78 milliseconds
alpha and gamma radiation

Radon 219 – 3.96 seconds
alpha and gamma radiation

Radium 223 – 11.43 days
alpha and gamma radiation

Thorium 227 – 18.7 days
beta and gamma radiation

Actinium 227 – 21.77 years
alpha and gamma radiation

Protactinium 231 – 32,760 years
beta and gamma radiation

Thorium 231 – 25.52 hours
alpha and gamma radiation

Uranium 235
703.8 million years

for all the bereaved

I

The pilots got sick in the air . . . They would report, calmly and simply, 'This will require two or three lives. And this, one life.'

Sergei Sobolev

THE MAN BURIED WITH CHERNOBYL

He's there. You might even see him – if you look
hard with X-rays. You could slice him like an embryo,

ply the great toothed wheel as it thrums with water – feed
cooling-water down the long shaft in an umbilical cord

of transparency, as though glass had come to life
twisting around steel. Then stack each concrete wafer

to count it with Geigers: map his contours in roentgens,
reconstruct him in glowing 3D. He might almost be

recognisable to his wife. Perhaps he would stir – lift
from his calcined mould like a grit jelly. Step off the VDU

imagining himself the corpse at the end of a play
leaving behind the murdered outline in white carbon.

ANSWERS

Where are we going?
Where we will send you.

What will we do there?
What you are told.

How bad will it be?
No worse than it is.

Why did you pick me?
Because you were called.

How long will you keep us?
As long as it takes.

But how will you pay me?
With a shovel.

Whom do we meet there?
Your good selves returning.

What shall we tell them?
Nothing at all.

UKRITYE

Even the robots refuse. Down tools. Jerk up
their blocked heads, shiver in invisible hail. Helicopters

spin feet from disaster, caught in that upwards cone
of technicide – then ditch elsewhere, spill black running guts.

Not the Firemen. In rubber gloves and leather boots
they walk upright, silent as brides. Uppers begin

to melt. Soles grow too hot for blood. Still they shovel
the graphite that is erasing marrow, spine, balls –

that kick-starts their DNA to black and purple liquid life.
Then the Soldiers. Nervous as children. They re-make it –

erect slabs with the wide stare of the innocent, crosshatch
the wreck roughly with steel, fill it in with that grey

crayon of State Concrete. In soiled beds, in the dreams
of their mothers, they liquefy. Yet Spring still chooses

this forest, where no deer graze and roots strike upwards.
Fissures open in the cement – rain finds them. They grow:

puff spores of poison. Concrete and lead can only take
so much. What remains must be done by flesh.

SOLDIER

They gave us underwear. Socks, real leather boots.
Shoulder boards, trousers, two belts, shirts, a pack and cap.

This week I have to work on top. They call me *stork*.
The farmers say – *Where are the crickets? The slugs?*

but still something glistens in their gardens. Cherry
with each leaf perforated. Green lacework trees.

The old women scrub our clothes. Bend till their palms
blister, dissolve. They tell us – *It is not the soap.*

On concrete steps, in the shade of lintels – a fine
shimmer. Like finest snow. A ginger kitten

stretched in a kitchen window, its head a dried
apricot. One old man was weeding, the very

day he had to leave. *Why do you do that?* I asked.
Because he said, *that is the work you do*

in the summer. That's how it is as a soldier.
Those peasants. Painting door-planks and fences with

parting notes: *'10 May. Dawn. By donkey and cart.'*
'May 24. There is pilaf in the blue pan.'

'Don't kill our Zhuchok. He's a good dog – 4ᵗʰ June.'
'June 1ˢᵗ. Forgive us, house.' On the walls their photos

tilt – as though the rooms were trying to recall them.
One village had spilled out a wedding, the bride's

red lips barely kissed, and we were removing
topsoil. Spraying foam. Now the looters have started –

pink candy crushed on asphalt. Their currency
of bottles. What can we do? Chernobyl has left,

gone from the map. To flea markets, second-hand stores,
dachas. One man, they say, bought a pillbox hat –

you know, black market. Had to watch his wife's head
grow the black brim. No joke. Our captain. Sleeps with his

Geiger under the bed. A woman came past
playing the accordion. *Where did you get that?*

he barks. Prods his Tube at her keys as though It
could smell music. *Bury it. Now.* Her mouth – just like

my mother's when she saw the letter's red stripe
and knew what it meant. That's fine – I wanted to stop

bullets with my chest. But these bullets are as strange
as needles. And this, a strange war. You get killed

when you get back. Most nights I hear my mother's voice,
my grandmother's. Doctor says – *It's the heat. Just*

wash your hands before eating. Today I get
my commendation. Some hero! Always nodding.

The boys lift me onto their shoulders. Take slugs
of vodka. Twelve each. Today at the reactor

I will have my picture taken.

MINERS

We worked naked. The old way.
A shovelful – sometimes a handful

at a time. Every mineshaft pisses itself.
But this – this one stank. Something

wrong in the water. And that heat.
As if there was more Earth above you

than below. We came out fainting
like girls. Our black wouldn't wash.

We knew this was no ordinary ore.
That each grain we dug was worth a life.

We lived for morning. How it gave
delicate colour to the walls of our tunnel.

They filled it with mercury-water –
it thrashed at the sides as Holy Water

in some vein of hell. *Liquid air*
they said. *Or this Reactor will sink*

like Atlantis. And now there are those
who will not stand near us. To them

I say – *How will you bury us?* And so
we are all agreed. All we brothers –

from Kiev. Moscow. Dnepropetrovsk.
We vow to bury one another. *This*

is impossible they tell us. *It cannot*
be done. It can. We are miners.

We know how to dig.

SLEEPWALKERS

How slow they move – these young women
in the twilight of a corridor. They do not

speak. Do not eat or drink. Just shower
then towel themselves down. Shower again.

Their eyes – too wide. They have seen
that strange light. Have walked the long dusk

in two long lines for that blurred vision
of showers. They are as women paying

respects at the bright coffin of themselves.
A line shuffles out. Scrubbed and carbolic

in army pyjamas, the odd glimpse of satin
tied at the ankles. A line shuffles in – golems

of fabric with strings dragging like broken
legs of spiders. Each hauls her carapace

of jaundice and purple – rubber and iodine –
the colours of sleep. In slippers, gumboots.

Hobnails, trainers. Yet none makes a sound.
The men are watching, secret and sad. Watch

without speaking as the women shower –
towel themselves down. Then shower again.

GREY MEN

They thicken to a second skin – grow on us –

our clothes. A grey rind. Only teeth show through. Our
teeth only. White and shining and in the moment.

Today a man with a box and shoulder strap
waved his wand over our empty boots. Jumped back.

Our poor boots – transfigured. A new kind of black.
We pity them and drink all night. Vodka, moonshine,

aftershave. Lacquer. Grigory says humankind
grew from fungus. I say we Russians are from

a different mould. We arrived full-grown.

*

That reactor, says Ivan, *is deliverance.*
Will spawn new words. Chernobylite. I tell him

they will hang us like overalls on his new words –
so they can always find us and put us away.

Ivan is shaking his big head. *But think*, he says,
of our genius children. They will be called

out of bed by their friends. Just to see them stand
there in nightclothes, a pale blue ember. A splinter

of dawn.

*

We are men who would talk about Time

on Death Row. Time that is inside out –
the old who want to live forever

our children who think only of death.
We salute wives. Other planets. Then kill

the lights. We move to our bunks – slow squid
in a moonlit ocean. Our milked bodies

pulse to get between the sheets. We have
hung our skins, our human skins where we

can find them. Grey men. Against the tall
windows – our line of grey men dozing

under their caps, backs to tomorrow's
firing squad of light. They stand without us.

Have everything they need from us.

MAY DAY

It is Spring. And every thing
        is on the move. In the meadow
                a cricket grates its tiny washboard

but his is a tune no female knows.
        A cow barges the gate whose bolt
                longs to slide. Whose hinge to squeal.

Back legs give way – she slips
        on a bloated udder and in its socket
                her great eye rolls. It is Spring. Things

still move. Bees drop short of the hive
        whose queen turns circles no worker
                can decipher. A toad lifts his solemn head

at the rim of a pond of foam. Rain falls.
        Is falling. This is Spring. Everything.
                His skin smells the scum. Smells it again.

SPRING

It is May Day. The children
    are eating painted eggs. Look

        at the fine colours. Pink and green
    for May Day. The workers

are marching. The men look
    fine. The sky is fine. The grass

        magnificent. This is May Day.
    A child is crying. Her cry is

natural. In her genes. She cries
    even though the rain falls pink

        and green on May Day. The veteran
    pats her parted hair – *Isn't that smell magnificent?*

She cries. And his face is a mask
    for May Day. May Day. May Day.

CHERNOBYL WEDDING

They hose down each cherry tree. Hose down
        the dogs. Mow the cemetery. Peel back the earth.

The guests arrive – they hose down the bus.
        The priest wears a mask. His faithful turn

to hymn number nought. No one mentions
        sickness or health. The groom bends to sign

in a flourish of white. No witness has seen it.
        Bells in the steeple swing without tongues.

Instead of confetti – foam. The bride's bouquet is
        caught mid-flight. And hosed. In the marquee

they scrape at pristine plates. The cellists
        draw bows across cello-shaped air. Father rises

to say nothing. The best man stands to deliver
        no joke. A Marshal marshals them tight to a lens –

orders a grin. No film. There is a black plastic
        bin-bag the gifts go straight in. He hands her a rose

in its hazard-tape bow. Their cake is sleek and black
        and melting. Past a colonnade of poplars drenched

in foam Wife and Man run. They are pulling them down.
        Guests huddle in their wake. Wave at an empty street.

FENCE

This side of the fence
is clean. That side
dirty. Understand?

You must forget
that soil is like skin.
Or interlocking scales

on a dragon. Dirty
Clean – is all that matters
here. Imagine a sheet

of glass coming down
from the sky. It's easy
no? On this side

you can breathe
freely. Your cow can
eat the grass. You can

have children. That side
you must wear a mask
and change the filter

every four hours.
You ask – What if my cow
leans over the fence?

Personally I say
it depends which end. But
we have no instructions

for that. It is up to you
to make sure your cow
is not so stupid.

POWDER / STONE

In our country it is not people you see
        but the powers that bind them. And

those are invisible. See how the film
        they bring back is black – their pictures

all black. They tried to repaint our village
        but whichever shade they chose came out

black. Their tapes are hiss. The radio
        hiss. Their videos are white noise

without the noise. Hear how the phone
        clicks into silence. Notice how there are

no orders. So take this powder. Make
        no fuss. Be silent as a fish. You could

have an accident. Quietly. You could
        be put in a room. A quiet room

where they say – *Take this powder*. So
        take it. Think like a stone. Be silent

as a she-fox wrapped around its cubs.
        Listen. I saw it – sitting in a chair

in an empty house. A black calf
        with hair to the ground. It was

eating stones. Its black eyes shone.

FISH STEW

Look. Here is a maid
milking. Observe. The Counter

by the teat of the cow
gives no sound. This bowl

of fish stew. Bought moments
ago from an open-air kiosk.

Not a click. These babies
pink as piglets squirming

in the sand. Note the twigs –
the stones in their mouths.

Do they cry? This woman
shrunk in bed to the size

of a child. That infant
whose blood separates

like soup. Nothing. Nothing
at all. Here is a family who

smelled the smoke. Do
the graves make a murmur?

And here. A man chewing
soft fuel from the reactor –

watch how his eyes spark
like firecrackers. Yet

the Geigers in his mouth
and rectum barely register.

Look. You can see
for yourselves. See

how rumours are
dangerous. This

is a fact.

TWO NEIGHBOURS

They tell us – bury
your cucumbers. You –
you eat them.

You were not in the War.

So for you Chernobyl
is less than a cucumber.

It was a good crop.

You feed them to your sons?
Your daughters?

They taste the same. No one
glows in their beds.

You are Thomas. Believe
only your eyes. Your stomach.

You believe too much.

But did you not feel it?
As if someone had opened
a tap in your side and let
all the life run out.

If you put it like that.

And our children. You ask them
to carry a pot – they take two
steps and crumple as if all
the air went from them.

If you put it that way.

You think men in suits
will take us to a bubble
on the moon?

My friend. Do not look
left or right. Right
or left.

And where did you look
when the rain was black –
the pine needles red?

My friend. They have
suits. They have instruments.
What do I have?

You have yourself.

At last
you understand.

I do not. You play music.
The whole world
rattles
and you play music?

So we will die
dancing.

RITE

Bring out the sack of wheat.
Scatter it in the garden.
Yes. Do as I say.

Throw all the eggs out
into the yard. I know – they
will break. But even

the fox must eat. Cut up
that last scrap of bacon.
For the cat. Take all

the seeds – cucumber,
carrot. Beetroot, swede.
I said take them

all out. Loose them
under the clouds – let them
be wild again. So they

can one day lift pale heads
through sleet and look
around them. Perhaps

they will look for us.
Soon we will be as close
to the earth as they. Do not

shake your head – do this
for me. Do it for yourself. So
we will have friends to meet us.

DIRECTIVE 1 A

those men
still warm from their beds
with the smell of their women
clinging to them – just like '37

bury them

the heads
of cabbage pulsing
thick veins
the turnip and carrot
the grain in its ears
the slim flowered dress
and wedding band

under white sand

that old woman sick
in her cot who rose
to meet the men in suits
yellow as devils yet
out she stepped
to raise her stick

bury her quick

the fireman in gumboots
his heelprint in fuel
lads ragged with rays
carrying the flag
straight into hell
each figure that is
a walking root
dripping gas and
speaking grit

all in plastic and into the ditch

the head of the commune
secretly rich the peasant
on all fours digging
with a spoon the bandit
the Major the clown
and buffoon

eight foot down

the milkchurn full of moonshine
that milkmaid spitting rust
the 'we're going to the circus'
so her child will climb the truck

dig to the rock

the sparrow without branch
or byre the magpie and crow
seeking windshield and tyre
the chick in its nest only half
grown the grub the larva
the cat and the hound
the beetle the spider
still in its web the doe
and the vixen the wolf
and the roe the forest the
treetops the rivers and
air the mountains the
oceans the planets and
spheres the seasons the
cosmos the race to
the moon

make a sarkophágos –
bury them

soon

I I

If the scientists know nothing, if the writers
know nothing, then it's for us to help them
with our lives and our death.

Voices from Chernobyl

'My parents kissed – and I was born.'

Then black clouds. Black rain.
Our garden all white. Not a white
like snow – but glass. We lived
in the cellar. Grandma told me to
count my sins – in case the devil
burst through the bricks with all
his heat behind him. I saw that frog
me and Vadik burst with a stick. How
its insides came out red like the jam I
dropped that made mama swear.

Dad came home black. Not his
clothes. His face. He said he got
too close. We visited him in a white
room. A man chased Kitty with a Geiger.
Tried to put the clicks on Kitty's tail
like salt. He had a big plastic bag. Got
angry when I giggled – when I shouted
Run Kitty! When we saw Dad I told
the story. Then he got angry too.

Some old women met the train
when we stopped. They threw
brown stones at us. Then we saw
it was bread. One had a face like
Grandma. But when I asked for water
she made the sign of the cross. Took
one step back. A woman in a white
apron brought us ice cream. She let us
keep the glass. Then soldiers came –
kept washing our train. I looked for
the old woman. The one who looked
like Grandma. But she was gone.

39

A man in a white spacesuit and mask
met us at the hospital. He said – *Put
all your clothes in this bag*. I thought
about Kitty. I didn't laugh. He said
he was a doctor but I didn't believe him.
He didn't look like the doctors you see
in the films. Mama tried to keep her ring.
He shook his head. Told her something
about half a life. I was crying but happy
I would see the city. From the window
the city was grey. Now if a bee stings
you die. At night I look out the window
to see if there is a fox with three tails.
I will go to sleep. Like Dad. Dad
said we will all sleep forever.
And become science.

I dreamed I was dead – but
mama was crying in the dream.
She cried so loud it woke me up.
She woke me up so I wouldn't die.
But when I looked around for her
she wasn't there. They take me to her
on Tuesday. *Remember – she can't
talk*. That's what he says. The man
who thinks he is a doctor. But he's
wrong. Mama speaks to me. She
does. With her eyes. Mama told me –
We all come back as someone else.
Vadik told me my parents kissed
and I was born. I will find a boy
in the ward. A boy like Vadik.
And kiss him.

They put me in a white room.
To paint. No one hugs me.
Under the window is a nest.
I wait to see if there are babies.
To see if the daisies will open –
if they are black. A woman with
red hair looks at what I paint.
She sits with her hands folded.
Says her name is not important.
I make a painting and she holds it
up to the window. Like X-rays.
She says – *Are all your people
black?* I don't answer. I twist
my brush in the paint. The way
Dad would do with his fork
with noodles. I pick up as much
of the dark as I can. I ask him
for more – the man who pretends
to be a doctor. I tell him. *There
is never enough black.*

SOURED MILK

I scrubbed the floors. Whitewashed the stove.
Left a loaf, salt on the table. Brought earth

from my mother's grave. Put it in a saucepan
and covered it. On my grandfather's mantel

I set a bowl and three spoons. Mikhail. Olya.
Nadezhda. So the three of you would return.

I wrote our names on the fence. On the hearth
– on logs. Along the asphalt of the road.

I would have written on scampering beasts
if they had lived. How silent our yard was.

They executed dogs. Callously, like spies.
Their eyes said – *Be grateful we do not shoot*

you. Our roosters grew black combs. Looked
like emperors. Then died. The old ones leant

forward in their beds, back into our time. *Drink*
vodka, they croaked. *For God's sake. Drink.*

Here the daughter-in-law follows me round.
Wipes the doorknob. The chair. Everything

I reach for. Scolds the dog for licking my cheek.
She says, I sour the milk. This city – where

they keep a hammer behind the front door.
My girls – I weep to have your father. Even

his footprint. A woman can wait for a man
to return from the forest. But never the earth.

Remember. On the day you carry me out don't
bump me against the mirror. Don't touch me

against the door. Or it will draw to those walls
another corpse. Do what I say, and I will see you.

When you put me in that box and burn me
stand five minutes. Do as I ask. Stand and think

of the house where you were born.

GOLUBOY

Camera crews interview
the other couples. Never us.
Out in the square the men

swivel as we pass. Mumble
goluboy – but with no laughter
in it. They blame the radiation –

dogs and cats are running
together. Boys are netting fish
without fins. Newborns arrive

with yellow blood. And now
this. We have become to them
all too plain. Together we lose

our hair. Lose our fingernails.
With each day our complexion
grows towards the moon. Me

and my Mal'vina. As death nears
it makes us twin. You know
– that reactor was worth it

almost. Now we can dance
down our street unmolested.
Now it is we who radiate

power. And *then* – then
the miracle. No. Not our
cells rejuvenated. But my

father. Out of the pale blue
my father. He met no eye. Said
no word. But stepped up just

the same. Out of that huddle
to shake my hand. To nod
goodbye. And so we two

have this world to ourselves.
They dare not risk their boots
on us. Fear to their marrow

what might be exchanged
between us in an insult.
Or a glance.

IVAN

She packed our baby and left.
    Bitch. I won't string myself up like

Viktor. Won't step out of a window.
    When I got back a year before

with a suitcase of roubles it was
    darling darling. The apartment –

she chose it. A bedroom with glass
    in the ceiling. We soldiers had a song:

The Geiger counters click and whine
    But oh we get it up each time.

Want to hear a joke? A man comes
    home from Chernobyl. His wife runs

straight to the doctor. *What can I*
    do with him? she asks. *First wash him*

says the doctor. *Next take him*
    to bed. Then deactivate him. Bitch.

I didn't cry. Not for her. Went straight
    to a party. Found a girl. *What's*

the point? she said. *You're Chernobyl.*
    Out there they took my crucifix

and hung a Geiger round my neck.
    Had to switch it off to make myself

heard. *Put a spoonful of goose shit*
  in vodka. That's what they said. *Let it*

stand two days. Drink it. We had
  another song – *What's a few roentgens*

between comrades? What's a few roentgens
  between friends? Those testicles

in suits won't let me have my file. See –
  exiled even from my own secrets.

You too. With your microphones.
  That pity in your eyes like small print.

And her. I'll show her I could survive
  at the centre of the sun. Breathe that heat

like perfume. Won't give her the pleasure
  even of making me bitter. Bitch –

all of you. I'll marry. Raise an army.
  I'll be Russia's fucking Abraham.

'Can you eat apples from Chernobyl?'
'You can, but be sure to bury the cores deep in the ground.'

Radio Armenia

In this part of the world
we make do. I sell apples.
Big. Red as a baby's head.

Apples! I call. *Buy apples*
from Chernobyl! My sister
tells me I am a fool. *Who*

will eat your apples? she asks.
Half of Moscow, I reply. *Bosses.*
Mothers-in-law. Bad teachers.

BREATHING

They had to teach me
from scratch. Teach me

       to breathe. As though
       I had fallen out of space or

up from water and breath
was labour – each breath

       a pang to draw me back
       from the brink. In. Out. In

this world life is indifferent.
You must will it in. Will it

       out. I look at my son –
       those white cheeks that

tight frown and
I wonder how I can

       breathe. He says – *Mama*
       when you go to sleep to-

night please don't forget to
breathe. Please. He is

       not allowed to run. Or
       jump. Like that boy who

hanged himself with a
belt. I watch him. And he

       watches me – when I doze
       on the red sofa he rests a

hand to check the rise and
fall of my chest. Tells me he

      will teach me in his dreams –
      will teach me to breathe if

I teach him how to fly. *If*
you go with Grandpa he

      says – *will you be able to*
      breathe? He says this and

his cheeks run wet and
he runs short of breath so

      we sit once again to
      teach each other how —

deep and slow. *We are*
flying I tell him. *We are*

      breathing   he replies.

THIS

is something you cannot write.
That when lymph nodes are removed

the nose shunts sideways – bloats
to three times its normal size. How

eyes brim with an unfamiliar light
as though a stranger were using them

to see the world for the first time.
This is not something you can write.

That when he saw himself he rocked
in the bed – head between fists – swaying

just swaying beneath a column of pain
unable to gutter off even the slightest

part of it in a snarl or sob because
everything lung upwards was tubes.

No. Some things you can never write –
how no mirror can ever again show me

the face I once had with him. That
I have come to believe all mirrors

should be taken down with their curse
of silver linings and one by one

each lamp dimmed in case we catch
sight of what really happened. They say

You must write to the relatives. As if
he were some thing you could turn

into letters. And yet he drives ink
across those white steppes of journals –

dark swarming herds you can read
only with a mirror – in case. In case

this is something you cannot write.
Oh shut the book. Just shut it. All

its bright pages will turn back
to dirt. Then tell yourself

this   this is
something

TRANSPLANT

Side by side their worlds
went dark. Twin tables
almost touching.

One night short of her
thirtieth and she let them
needle her sternum – that

thick weld of ribs – filch
her bones for a tubful
of roe to seep into his.

A lottery ticket in blood.
But something salmon swam
against all her intentions.

Now at the edge of sleep
he turns to her. Says *sister*
with those filmy eyes.

They say she'll never
marry. Her blood
watered down. Yes –

choose when to visit
with care. One day her
thoughts are cased in zinc;

the next she flares green fire
East to West. Bellows –
You think that Reactor

knew about borders?
One woman whispers they
messed with her marrow

and now she's a witch.
Perhaps, drinks blood.
Sometimes with the light

behind her you could swear
you make out bones. Her
hollow bones. And always

in her eyes that look –
that drift back and forth
between our world and his.

FIRST LIGHT

I hear him. In that thin wash of dawn
when world is caught remembering
it ought to be real

and at the foot of your bed you glimpse
your night self spooling back its long trails
from each of the rooms.

That's when he walks. Walks those stairs
in my head and I wake – remember
I have a house.

On yellow sand they walk me. Where
there's as much sea as sky. I remember
there is no God.

I try to be water. What mostly makes us
makes us kin. Water can have a past.
Can remember.

A girl steps up. Says – *I've finished my
homework*. Unspoilt cheeks. Unnatural
blue eyes. And I raise

hands to a face sticky with myself. At last
I look through. Remember
I have a daughter.

OLYA

Little woman the nurses called her –
for the way she brought a lifetime's grace

to a child's demeanour, how when she
danced she hardly parted those feet –

her small weight so subtle from ball
to arch, heels barely lifting for each

quick surge she sent up her spine to
fountain arms and sprinkle fingers.

Later she began to move like that doe
they filmed returning from the reactor:

skinny and slowed into some other,
parallel time. I'd quarter fruit and she'd

refuse it. Near the end she drew nothing
but ballerinas. Beamed at visitors who

befriended her for articles and art
then never came back. Her sister says –

Two angels took her. One each hand.
I prefer facts to moondust. And yet

the intern shakes a methodical head, insists
that with her spine completely rotten

still the impossible happened. In that long
black sleep before she stopped – before

the machine's insolent bleep – those
wasted toes stirred. Practised steps.

THE ROOM

This hospital has a room

for weeping. It has no crèche.
No canteen. No washroom queue.

Only this queue for weeping.
No lost property booth. No

complaints department. Or
reception. No office of second

opinion. Of second chances. Its sons
and daughters die with surprise

in their faces. But mothers
must not cry before them. There is

a room for weeping. How hard
the staff are trying. Sometimes

they use the room themselves. They
must hose it out each evening.

The State is watching. They made
this room for weeping. No remission –

no quick fixes. A father wonders
if his boy is sleeping. A mother

rakes her soul for healing. Neighbours
in the corridor – one is screaming

It moved from your child to mine.
More come. Until the linoleum

blurs with tears and the walls
are heaving. Until the place can't

catch its breath – sour breath
of pine. And at its heart

this room.

'Every day I found a new man.' Ludmila Ignatenko.

Do not kiss him they said, starting back, as though
he were an animal in its cot cocking its head to listen

but understanding nothing. *Do you understand? Are you
pregnant? No? And find him milk. Three litres a day.*

I poured that whiteness into him. Felt I was feeding
a goose its own feathers. He retched and cursed –

the thin dribble each side of his mouth worse than a child.
Each time you hold his hand is a year off your life. Can you

hear us? His bones are more active than the Core.
Understand? That is no longer your husband. I boiled

chickens until the bones sagged, fresh, handfuls of parsley
chopped so fine it would melt between finger and thumb,

pot barley, apples (from Michurinsk they told me) pared
and pulped, everything minced and sieved, every trace

of rind or pip removed, no husk shell or pod and all of it
spewed back down his chest as though he could not take

a single particle more. The black of his forearms and thighs
cracked like pastry. His eyelids swelled so tight with water

he could not see for skin. The lightest sheet peeled away
fat as flypaper, the slightest edge of thumbnail was to him

more vicious than any cut-throat – if I moved his head it
streaked hair down the pillow as though he were a used match,

if I pressed a knuckle in – our wedding flesh – the indent
remained like hot grey putty, he coughed bile, acid

froth and lung, shreds of stomach and liver and still he
stayed – refused that first, that last, step onto the Jacob Ladder.

60

Those reptile eggs of eyelids, turned always towards me.
Until I said *Go. I love you. But Go.* Up to that moment

I still believed I would save him. Milk, soup, kisses. As if
he could digest the touch of my lips, feel my making of broth

in his dissolving heart-chambers. When his breath shut,
when he began to cool – then – I called for family. It was

almost a miracle, the Doctors said. Four times the fatal dose
and he nearly turned round. I felt myself the wrong side

of a door – a partition thin as plywood, thinner, as though
you could hear everything that was going on inside.

His mother hugged me. The brothers kissed me. *Now we
are your brothers.* Have you ever been the wrong side

of that door, knowing all you needed was the key and you
could walk straight in? That's how it was. We were that close.

III

Without the shadow of death
nothing can be understood.

Viktor Latun, photographer

A NAME

It was on the tram. So clear. A woman said
my name. There was no mistake. Said I was

dead. She was shopping. Telling a friend.
I got off the next stop. Opened the paper

and there it was. I've been walking to work
afraid to arrive. Would my place be blank –

my drawer emptied out? Would I find
another man in my chair? Another man in

my house? She gave my name. No mistake.
Now I'm standing on the pavement and no one

is looking. The whole street in blossom and
I can smell nothing. Is this what it is like

to be dead? Perhaps everyone inside that tram
was dead. And you. Do you know me? I must

find someone who knows me. Someone who
knows my name. Perhaps it is only my name

that died.

THE BREATH

Not impossible is it? Or even
                     unlikely. That a bus conductor

leaned from his step that day, craned
                     east round the corner of his pole

and took it. Or that a young woman
                     punching air with the news

of her promotion struck out
                     for an early lunch – much earlier

than she might have done – and
                     throwing her head back in triumph

took it. Or that a boy held his lolly
                     up to the sun for comparison and

at its resonant lemon – gasped.
                     And took it. Or that some incoming

dispatch crackled my radio which I
                     lifted to the sill (raising the sash

for better reception) which is why
                     I was standing by that open window

so under-informed – so maybe it was
                     me who took it, liable as any

conductor, woman, boy who didn't
                     take it at all, just me – half-cut with

the dusk for Christ's sake – bet it
        was, knowing my bum luck, knowing

me – when it might have sunk sizzling
        into the gutter or made some privet leaf

grow backwards or something – but
        the odds are still on my side – aren't

they? – with me, whose breath maybe
        didn't slide in that day with its fizzing

speck of cargo, to bank in my lung
        its bastard atom. So not me after

all? Not impossible. Is it. Or even
        unlikely? That I didn't? Didn't take

that one wrong breath.

ONE WORD

There was life – a life
            before. A girl of sixteen

a rigger of twenty-four
            meeting for cakes and

nothing else. A girl who
            made herself late just to

see what a handsome man
            waited for her. After

work. Beneath the clock
            close by the Post Office –

Volodarsky Street. And
            ah that night they shared

champagne and madeleines
            under stars in Gorky Park

until their hands gravitated
            and both dared whisper

yes. Yes they said – then
            touched lips as though it

were some law of physics.
            One year together before

finally they kissed – and
            nothing more. Who would

believe it? Who would
    change a breath of it? –

even if a voice of doom
    boomed in from the planets.

I keep that *yes* – folded in me
    tight and small as the slip

in a fortune cookie. *Yes* –
    one word I go on presenting

to myself as though I might
    one day hate what it says.

Yes. That last atom
    in me that is not

contaminated.

BABA NADYA

She weeps for the trees. Baba Nadya
comes to our village to weep for trees.

For that stiff gentleman poplar she keens.
For the bartender oak who leant – stout

at the fence. For big-headed walnut
and leprous birch she grieves. For the gaunt

Spanish chestnut – and the desperate
alder close to water where she clings

to frail fingers of long-haired willow.
Baba Nadya sags even for an elf

of hazel or pick-pocket rowan. Mark
the sprawling ash whose name she gobbles

like a familiar. See her crouch so close
to the ground her skirt is a bustle black

and round as a cauldron. Watch this woman
of wood whose eyelids redden at stumps

as though they were her children. And each
trunk that dies a coffin in the making.

CURATOR

She stood – huge in that oak doorway
hurling currency. *Here! Take back your*

blood money. Take it! Keep the medals.
The certificate. Give me my husband.

The walls shouted back – then rang
as if slapped. The glass cases felt it

and shivered. How could I speak
for a museum? For this handful of soil

under glass? Or this miner's helmet
in which poison has drilled so many

pot-shots? How to tell her I could not
mount even one photograph of the girl

who strolled that morning through dew
and made her legs a living sieve? That

was then. Now – this funeral parlour
in public. This is for when we have gone

the way of Aztec and Khazar. This is
because even forgetting needs a shrine.

Yes – they come. Gaze at her husband
behind glass. A medal. His careful notes.

Some weep. Perhaps it is because
they do not know what to remember.

But I see it. When the last has left
and there are only keys. Her mouth

gaping as if all air had turned to glass.

BLACK

In the dark   she goes to him
   for his crusts   of hipbone

       His weather maps   still
   Walls   Medals   A certificate

       That first   squirt of
   blood   sounds   the bedpan

       as milk sounds   the pail
       His own mother refuses

   At the end   of a tube
   they chart   the poppy-seed

       in his   lung   that splits
       straight into bloom

       He moults   black skin
       in shawls   spreads dark

   in the silhouette   of Lenin
   His livid   seed will   lodge

       in the   culs-de-sac
   of a dead village   He will

   go the way of water   Thinks
       of canal-weed   entering

   the slug   Knows   soon
   she will   feel in his urn

   for the intimate   shells
       of his death   He leaves her

       his fat   yellow watch
   Stress germinates it   She

wears black   And he   de-
  sires it Everywhere – black

        rips his bloodlines   B ursts
      fro m h im i n f i n e   j e t s

Those photos   down the hall
  – his own   camera crew

            who come   swooping
      to steer him   to stall his dark

Their booms track a whimper:
    Where is   Papa? Where

        exactly?   There are many
      rooms – Even the dead

  fear them

BLACK BOX

I was raw data. His something-for-nothing box.
   Caught him watching me as I slept – a cold

forensic look. He favoured a bed with bones
   that clicked. Wanted to see if my face was

different from the rest in the act of love.
   He'd inquire over dinner – jaw set in intense

nonchalance he thought I couldn't decipher –
   So. What colour did it burn? What colour

precisely? I turned the tables. Fed counterfeit
   stories to him as if I'd let slip – kept a diary

of the way his dessert spoon would hover mid-
   slurp – noted the lustre in those coins of eyes

as he made the base salute of a shirtsleeve dragged
   across lips, excused himself to the bathroom

to lick his stub of pencil, spend a breathless
   minute spawning apocrypha in that journal

jammed behind the cistern. God knows I'd tried –
   one dusk as the moon rose, thin as rice-paper

I ran true. Told him what I had seen there. Seen
   with my mind – that freedom is not an absence

of control. But he just leant closer as I blanched
   a perfectly good chicken in salt water then

threw out the scum – three times. Those monitor
   eyes widened. *Salt gets it out,* I told them.

I ditched him. Couldn't see then that he was right.
The Reactor – in me after all. A searing

rod of black so stuck in my crop it made me
fall for someone like him: grim receiver who'd

piece together my pain and publish the results.
Perhaps I hoped he'd draw it out – bloodied

from between my ribs. I'd rather he'd shoved it
home. Quelled this constant rising drone in my brain.

BOX

This room they wheel me to is
           an emptied box. *So* –
they grin: *what's the big story today*
           Viktor?   Children
they are. Children are always looking
           for stories. But I
tell it again. The one story in my head.
           ...Try to imagine
I say – *that steel rooms everywhere had*
           split their seams –
burst their box-buds open — swung
           four-square petals flat
to the ground. That from space
           every continent grew those
strange square stars sudden
           as an alpine meadow.   Watch
clipboarded men confer
           in levelled fields – their busy eyes
scaffolding vertices back
           into air. How gingerly they step
- awkward as roe - to that new
           edge of world vulnerable to
salvos of hail or blowing blossoms
           of paper. Such massive
exposure – and every bit unhinged
           as a doll's house in which
something not quite right has
           happened. See – the stacked
borders of fault analysis
           are losing their crisp definitions
to rain. Inspectors rap
           where a door once stood – flash
passes to a blank-faced sky.
           What next?   Who would be
first to press that button – snap
           the walls back up? Slam

the lid back on? How long before
                 the man at his console
forgets atoms must be constrained...
                 I run dry. They keep
filling in boxes.   Will never grasp
                 what fused in me – that
someone actually did it: opened a
                 box – that cracked idea of
a box – opened it right up and
                 turned our world – all of this
innocent unwalled world –
                 into one   Wrong–side–in · In–
side–up Down–side–out
                 admonishing chamber of gas.

α – β – γ

In Cloud Chamber
        they can seem quite

beautiful – that white
        sea-urchin of Alpha rays

whose imperative tracks
        of equal measure are so keen

to interact that when they
        strike they give their all – and

Beta rays which – observed
        at leisure in a supersaturated

vapour – are each a close-up
        end of overwashed hair –

and then we come to Gamma
        which can home in on

one strand of DNA and tie
        a knot in it that takes

generations to unravel
        Yes — all so beautiful

yet Alpha can do real
        mischief with the lining of

a stomach or bowel or
        pressed to lips — while Beta

ricochets bad luck from
        one watery room to the next

down those long corridors
        of cells — There are others

we may test: the positron for
        instance – or the neutrino

they call Ghost for the way
        it will glide unperturbed

through planets – though
        we shan't dwell on those

since we must return
  to Gamma: don't be fooled

by that track in the
  Chamber – as meagre and thin

as a child's scrawl –
  it is scattering skins of vicious

wavelength: is a rapier
  of radiation that runs clean

through a spine – several
      layers of steel — it will

find a way through – its
      wriggle of quantum

world always out
      to lance an egg

or top and tail a gene
      So – this then is our

little theatre: $\alpha - \beta - \gamma$
      These three will grace us

in goose-bump and bone:
  in a Geiger-Müller detector

or Scintillator they know
  their place – there we can see

what they do — but the
  Body: ah the Body is difficult

– is that new space of
  liver eye and testis – an occult

laboratory painted all
      puce and purple where no

permit is available – But
      it is still in our power

to wait – Oh Yes — we can
      wait for results

NANA

*nana?   what is
radiation?*   Ah – it is

everywhere.   All
around us.

*but nana   can you
see it?*

No.
can you smell it?

No.
can you touch it?   is it

hot?   No
my matryushka.

*but i can taste it   i think
i can   can you*

taste it nana?
Perhaps.   But I am

buried deep.
nana   i think i heard it

*in a dream
a teeny voice in my ear*

*all scratchy
and silly   like our radio*

that never worked
And what did it say?

*i don't know   i couldn't
hear*

80

Never mind. Sleep now –
go to sleep. I am tired.

nana   can we count the numbers
together?

Alright. Are you ready?
anna   eva   vasily

alexandr   mikhail   sofia
anastasia   nikolai

– nana   did i remember
them all?

Yes. Now close your eyes.
It is time to sleep.

nana   tell me
is radiation

like god?

THE CHAPEL OF THE VIRGIN MARY

Here. In forever twilight.
    The faint caesium glow

of her cape. Face white
    with lead. Those decades

strung along her rosary's
    suspension of atoms – how

they snag the small light!
    Miraculous – one tear

starts down her cheek –
    heavy water. That

bent finger she points
    to a porcelain heart.

And always her eyes –
    the way they tilt to where

an infant might rest – that
    bloodless cradle which is

her hollow of breast. Now
    old ones say – *See her*

and die. All who kneel
    here know. She too

once held a child
    that would not cry.

SHADOW

She came. I just know she
came. At nightfall I'd place

our boy's wet things under
her pillow. Each morning

they were dry and folded.
I contrived once – to stay

awake. Saw her slow shape
cast by the moon. Saw it

pass a shoulder-bone of wall.
His cot. Those tiny fists

shadow-boxing the dark.
I called her – but had left

the key in the door so
she vanished. I can't be

sure – even now – if that
first small cry came from

the boy. Outside was all
moon and snow. And nothing

to give him. Nothing. Just
my thumb to suckle.

BASHCHUK

In a dream he has
no shoes. He tells me
Buy slippers. The largest

you can find. Put them
on the lid of a coffin with
my name inside. Write

Bashchuk on a slip of paper
and put it inside. I will
find them. We are all

in the same place here.
I see his grey stumps.
Their ten clouded lenses

of toenail. *Elephant*
he says. *I am an elephant.*
Forget nothing. You must not

forget. Give me back
my flesh. They stole it
from me. Find my flesh.

Once he sighed – *Man shoots*
but God carries the bullets.
What now? How grey

his feet. How heavy.
And the skin wrinkled
like freshly poured lead.

He says – *Here cats eat*
tomatoes. They eat kittens
to purge themselves.

The dog waits at the gate
for his master – nothing
but ear and bone. Did they

lay me on the door
of our house – my brothers?
Did I die? And now

our daughter. Her hairless
body. Oh love. I am all
bone. Bring me slippers.

LAST WISH

You bury me in concrete. Bury me
in lead. Rather I was buried
with a bullet in the head.

You seal me in powder. Cut the hair
last. Then take the trimmings
and seal them in glass.

You wrap me in plastic. Wash me
in foam. Weld the box airless
and ram the box home.

For each tomb that's hidden a green
soldier turns. None decomposes.
Nothing for worms.

A buckle. A pencil. Break one thing
I left. Give some small part of me
ordinary death.

PRIPYAT

A cart. Neck broke. Head down. Both arms in the air.

A door. Secure – but four walls ajar. In line on the doorstep: three three-litre jars. Stretched triplicate mouths upturned. Perfect as choirboys'. Their parched lips ring with light: wine-glass sun's one yellow note.

The yard a black sea. Scorched by frost. But just there – the pale periscope of a beansprout.

A mailman's bike. Weedbound to a fence. The easy eyes of its chain: grass-threaded. Its flaccid bag and flap abrim with a trembling of beaks. Three yellow beaks. Fanfaring sun with fledgling nervous nothings.

EXPOSURES

So. What will it be? Picture it on that reel
inside your head. Do you see purple-red bluffs

of flame? What do you hide there? Incandescence
pushing unstoppably through troposphere? Bodies

making causeways for survivors? Who slipped those
pixels in? What if – instead – it's a vixen

stepping up to lick your fist? Or a circle
of rags black against snow? Perhaps it's going out

for papers and finding all the pages blank.
Or a cage hung out among pines – the squeamish

hinge – its parrot offering the forest tea.
Could it be the world shedding itself skin by skin

till a snotty-faced boy picks it up – shrugs then
pockets it – *because*? Just because there's no one

around and it fits so snug in his hand.

ENVOY

Take our words. Enrich them.
They are already active – but enrich them.

This is dangerous. May even be impossible.
They are dispersed through a great mass

and you may need to quarry this vastness
to elicit one bald grain. You may have

to detach yourself. Use robots and machines.
But at the end – after immense effort – you

will forge from our cries a single silver rod.
You will put it on display behind a screen.

Your scientists will marvel. Your politicians
quake. You will have to control and subdue it –

contain it with great care. Many will not wish
to have it near them. Or their children. You will

protect yourselves with suits. Put your ear to it
and hear it hum. It will make you shudder.

One night – in early darkness. When you are
thinking of something else.   It will escape.